How to Use the Tajweed Signs in Qur'an Recitation

اصطلاحات ضبط المصحف

A Guide on How to Use the Punctuation and Tajweed Signs to Recite the Qur'an with Proper Tajweed

Ayman Fathallah Hamed

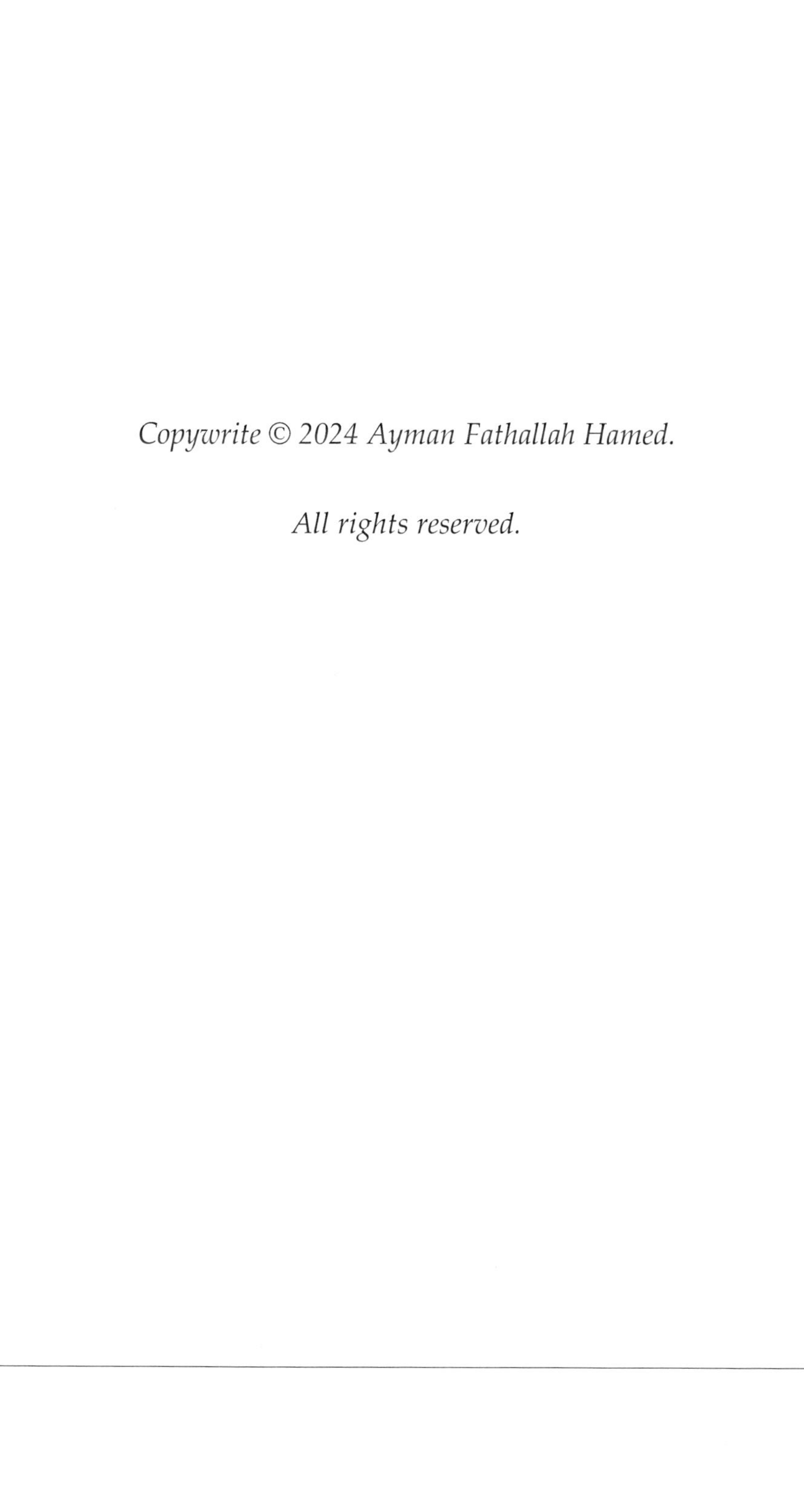

Table of Contents

INTRODUCTION

بسم الله الرحمن الرحيم

الحمد لله رب العالمين والصلاة والسلام على سيدنا محمد أشرف الأنبياء والمرسلين وعلى آله وصحبه أجمعين.

Allah (سبحانه و تعالى) commanded us to read the Qur'an, and He specified that we should read it with "Tarteel" (ترتيل). He said in Surat Al-Muzzamil (المزّمّل):

وَرَتِّلِ ٱلْقُرْءَانَ تَرْتِيلًا [1]

Tarteel of the Qur'an means to recite it clearly in a measured way. The measured way means that reciting the Qur'an has rules that differentiate it from other texts. The measured recitation requires pronouncing the letters clearly and properly while following the Tajweed rules (أحكام التجويد) and the stopping and starting rules (أحكام الوقف و الابتداء).

[1] Surat 73 (Al-Muzzammil): Aya 4

The Prophet Muhammad (صلى الله عليه وسلم) taught us, in many Ahadith (plural of Hadith in Arabic), the importance and the reward of learning and reading the Qur'an. The Messenger of Allah (صلى الله عليه وسلم) said:

"خيركم من تعلم القرآن وعلمه."

"The best among you are those who learn the Qur'an and teach it to others."

He also said:

" اقرؤوا القرآن فان لكم بكل حرف حسنة والحسنة بعشر أمثالها، أما إني لا أقول ألم حرف، ولكن ألف حرف ولام حرف و ميم حرف. "

"Read the Qur'an; you will be rewarded a "Hasana" (a good deed) for each letter, and Allah multiplies the reward ten times. I am not saying "Alif, Laam, Meem" is a letter, rather I am saying "Alif" is a letter, "Laam" is a letter, and "Meem" is a letter."

Meaning of Tajweed

To do Tajweed on something means to beautify it. The technical meaning of Tajweed is to articulate every letter from its articulation point with the proper attributes while maintaining the rights and dues of each letter.

Here is a quick explanation of the terms mentioned in the technical meaning of Tajweed:

- **Articulation point (مخرج الحرف)** is where the letter comes out when we pronounce it.
- **Attributes of the letter (صفات الحروف)** are the properties that distinguish each letter, like heaviness or lightness of the letter, or the Ghunna (الغنّة), which is the nasal sound that comes out when we pronounce the letters " م , ن ".
- **Rights of the letter** are the features *required* for each letter; without them, it is broken or not the same letter anymore. **Dues of the letter** are the features ***needed for perfecting the pronunciation but*** changing them will not change the letter. For example, stretching the letter Alif (ا) (in its natural

length) to 2 counts is a *"right"*, if you cut it shorter then it is no longer an Alif; while if you don't pronounce a heavy letter (like ص or ط) with proper heaviness, you take away a *"due"* of the letter, which doesn't change it, but it is not the perfect way of pronunciation.

ABOUT THIS BOOK[2]

Learning to read the Qur'an has many stages; it includes learning the Arabic Alphabet, the articulation points of the letters (مخارج الحروف), the attributes of the letters (صفات الحروف), the rules of stopping and starting (أحكام الوقف و الابتداء), and the Tajweed rules (أحكام التجويد).

When the Ayat of the Qur'an were written down at the time of Prophet Muhammad (صلى الله عليه وسلم), they were written without using the dots on letters, because at that time, Arabs were able to recognize the letters and the words from the context of the sentence. Later on, the dots on the letters were introduced, making it easier, especially for non-Arab Muslims, to understand the Qur'an.

---

[2] Note: Please make sure to read this section carefully before continuing to the Signs and Rules section.

Muslims throughout the centuries have given great attention to serving the Qur'anic text. Nowadays, the Qur'anic text not only has dots on the letters but also signs or symbols on the words or between the Ayat and the Suras. Those signs and symbols provide guidance and hints on how to read the Qur'an with the basic Tajweed rules. Those signs and symbols are collected in **The Convention of Dabt Signs (اصطلاحات ضبط المصحف**), which can be found at the end of the Mus-haf (المصحف).

Note that:

- The Mus-haf (المصحف) is the book that contains the Holy Qur'an. So, the Qur'an is the collection of the Ayat and the Suras that were revealed to the Prophet Muhammad (صلى الله عليه وسلم), while the Mus haf is the book in which they are written down.
- Dabt (ضبط) means punctuation and making things precise.

The Convention of Dabt Signs is a key to understanding the punctuation and Tajweed signs used in the Qur'anic text. ***This book is intended to guide you in learning how to use those punctuation and Tajweed signs to apply the basic Tajweed rules when reciting the Qur'an. Following those punctuation and Tajweed signs should allow you to apply many basic Tajweed rules, even without fully understanding them.***

Learning Tajweed should be done by attending Tajweed classes conducted by qualified teachers, and from Tajweed books. This book is intended to be used as a guide for understanding the punctuation and Tajweed signs in the Qur'anic text, and it is not meant to be a book for learning Tajweed rules.

It is recommended to have a basic background in Tajweed before using this book. For example, you are expected to know what Idgham, Ikhfa', and the other Tajweed rules are, and this book will guide you on how to use the signs in the Qur'anic text to perform the Tajweed rules properly.

Using the punctuation and Tajweed signs to apply the Tajweed rules should not be considered a replacement for the traditional way of learning Tajweed. Still, it can be considered a simplified method to perform many of the Tajweed rules just by following the signs in the text.

Let's look at some examples to have an idea about how to use those signs so we can understand what this book is about:

- **Example (1):**

- Look at the letter "نْ" in the following Aya:

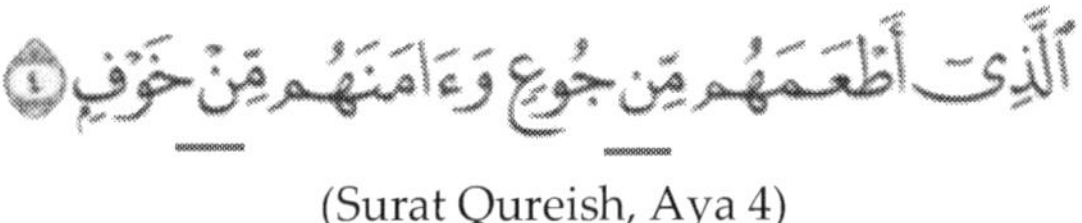

(Surat Qureish, Aya 4)

The letter "نْ" (underlined in the example above) was written one time without any marks (it was left blank), and the second time it was written with a Sukoon " ْ ".

- In the next Aya, the letter "ن" was written without any marks but there is a Shadda " ّ " on the next letter:

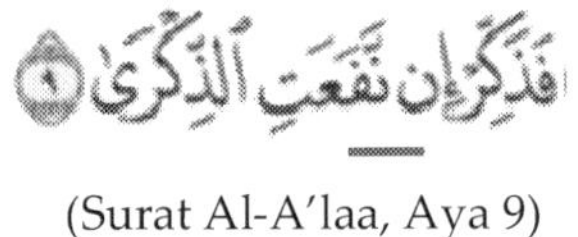

(Surat Al-A'laa, Aya 9)

- What is the significance of writing the same letter " ن " in different ways?

- **Example (2):**

- Look at the Tanween in the following Aya:

(Surat Al-Ghaashiya, Aya 2)

- Why is the same Tanween (underlined in the example above) written in two different ways?

- Also, the same Tanween is written in the next Aya in another way:

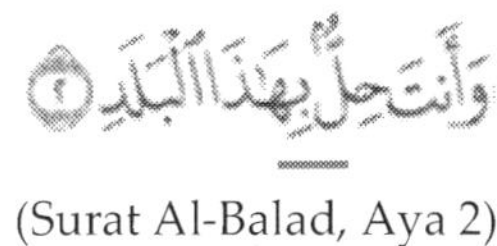

(Surat Al-Balad, Aya 2)

In this book, in sha Allah we will be answering those questions and more. We will discuss and analyze the punctuation and Tajweed signs so we can learn how to use them to perform many of the basic Tajweed rules.

Benefits of This Method

When we learn Tajweed in the traditional way, we discuss the letters of the Arabic Alphabet and how the Tajweed rules affect each one of the 28 letters. For example, the Noon Sakina (نْ) has four rules (Idgham, Izhar, Ikhfa', and Qalb). In the traditional way, we learn how to apply each one of the four rules based on the letter following the Noon Sakina.

Practically, after we learn the Tajweed, we notice that the Noon Sakina will be pronounced in one of the following four ways:

- Pronounced clearly
- Replaced with a Ghunna (a nasal sound)
- Totally dropped
- Converted into Meem (م)

Each one of the above four ways of pronunciation is ***marked*** in a certain way in the Qur'anic text. In this book, we will learn how to recognize those marks and punctuation in order to apply the proper Tajweed rules even if we don't have prior knowledge of which Tajweed rule is supposed to be applied.

SIGNS AND RULES

The signs that will be discussed in this book are based on Mus-haf Al-Madina (مصحف المدينة), with Riwayat Hafs 'an 'Asim (رواية حفص عن عاصم). This book also contains a few signs from Mus-haf of Kuwait (مصحف دولة الكويت), which is also based on Mus-haf Al-Madina (مصحف المدينة), but with some additions and variations on the signs and the symbols. Please note that the terms "marks" and "signs" will be used interchangeably for the signs discussed in this book.

For each sign, you will find ***a photocopied snippet***, from the original Convention of Dabt Signs. Each one of the snippets includes an explanation in Arabic on how to use the sign and some examples. A ***transliteration*** is also provided for each given example. Also, for many of the Tajweed terms, you will find the Arabic meaning provided next to the English term. This should be useful for anyone who wants to get familiar with the terms of Tajweed in Arabic.

Vowel Letter (ي , و , ا)

i. Small Circle (۠)

Having this sign (۠) on top of one of the vowel letters (ي , و , ا) indicates that this vowel letter is silent and should not be pronounced (whether you stop on it or continue reading), as shown in the examples below:

(Qaaloo) قَالُوا۟

(Yatlu suhufan) يَتْلُوا۟ صُحُفًا

(La'athbahannahu) لَأَا۟ذْبَحَنَّهُۥ

(Wa'ulul 'ilmi) وَأُو۟لُوا۟ ٱلْعِلْمِ

(Banainaahaa bi'aydin) بَنَيْنَٰهَا بِأَيْي۟دٍ

وضع الصفر المستدير (۠) فوق حرف علّة يدل على زيادة ذلك الحرف فلا يُنطق به في الوصل ولا في الوقف، نحو: ﴿ قَالُوا۟ ﴾ ، ﴿ يَتْلُوا۟ صُحُفًا ﴾، ﴿ لَأَا۟ذْبَحَنَّهُۥ ﴾، ﴿ وَأُو۟لُوا۟ ٱلْعِلْمِ ﴾، ﴿ بَنَيْنَٰهَا بِأَيْي۟دٍ ﴾.

Snippet from the original "**Convention of Dabt Signs (اصطلاحات ضبط المصحف)**"

ii. Small Oval (٥)

This sign (٥) on top of an Alif (ا) indicates that we should pronounce it only when we stop on it, but we drop it (it is silent) when we continue reading. Here are some examples:

(Ana khairum minhu) أَنَا۠ خَيْرٌ مِّنْهُ

(Laakinna Huwallaahu Rabbee) لَّٰكِنَّا۠ هُوَ ٱللَّهُ رَبِّي

ووضع الصّفر المستطيل (٥) فوق ألف بعدها متحرّك يدل على زيادتها وصلاً لا وقفاً، نحو: ﴿أَنَا۠ خَيْرٌ مِّنْهُ﴾ ﴿لَّٰكِنَّا۠ هُوَ ٱللَّهُ رَبِّي﴾

Snippet from the original "**Convention of Dabt Signs (اصطلاحات ضبط المصحف)**"

Note that, this sign is used when the letter after the Alif (ا) has a Haraka(◌ِ , ◌ُ , ◌َ) not a Sukoon[3]. If the letter after the Alif has a Sukoon, then the Alif is written without any signs, but it still follows the same rule as the Alif that has an oval (٥); (that

[3] The blank circle in(◌ِ , ◌ُ , ◌َ) is just a placeholder for letters.

is, we drop it when we continue reading, and we pronounce it when we stop on it).

- **Example:**

(Anan natheeru) أَنَا۠ ٱلنَّذِيرُ

So, there is a Saakin letter after the Alif, and there is no small oval sign on top of the Alif, but we still apply the above rule.

وأهملت الألف التي بعدها ساكن نحو:
﴿أَنَا۠ ٱلنَّذِيرُ﴾، من وضع الصفر المستطيل فوقها، وإن
كان حكمها مثل التي بعدها متحرك في أنها تسقط وصلاً
وتثبت وقفاً، لعدم توهم ثبوتها وصلاً.

Snippet from the original **"Convention of Dabt Signs (اصطلاحات ضبط المصحف)"**

Hamzat-ulwasl (همزة الوصل)

Hamzat-ulwasl (also known as Alif-ulwasl (ألف الوصل)) is a Hamza (or an Alif (ا)) that is added to the beginning of certain words in Arabic. Those words start with a Saakin letter (a letter that has a Sukoon).

In Arabic, you can't start speaking with a Saakin letter, so in case the first letter in a word happens to be a Saakin letter, Arabs add an Alif or a Hamza that is called Hamzat-ulwasl or Alif-ulwasl to the beginning of that word to allow for starting the sentence with it.

➔ **Hamzat-ulwasl or Alif-ulwasl in the Qur'anic text always has a small " ص " on top of it.**

Whenever we see a small " ص " on top of an Alif (ا) we know that it is a Hamzat-ulwasl, and it should be dropped (not pronounced) when it is in the middle of a sentence, but it is pronounced as a Hamza " ء " if you start the sentence with it.

Here is an example:

(Fa-ithan shaqqatis samaa'u) فَإِذَا ٱنشَقَّتِ ٱلسَّمَآءُ

> وَوَضْعُ رَأْسِ صَادٍ صَغِيرَةٍ هَٰكَذَا « ص » فَوْقَ أَلِفِ الوَصْلِ (وَتُسَمَّىٰ أَيْضًا
> هَمْزَةَ الوَصْلِ) يَدُلُّ عَلَىٰ سُقُوطِهَا وَصْلًا. مِثْلَ (فَإِذَا ٱنشَقَّتِ ٱلسَّمَآءُ)

Snippet from the original **"Convention of Dabt Signs (اصطلاحات ضبط المصحف)"**

➔ **Note: The Hamza at the beginning of the word can either be Hamzat-ulwasl (discussed above), or Hamzat-ulqat', which is written as (أ or إ) and is always pronounced.**

Lam Atta'reef (لام التّعريف)

Laam Atta'reef (لام التّعريف), which is sometimes referred to as Al-Atta'reef (ال التّعريف), is a Laam " ل " that is added to nouns to define them (make them definite). If I say (بيت) which means a house, this could mean any house, but if I say (البيت) then I define which house I am talking about. This is like using "***the***" in English.

Since this Laam is a Saakin letter (has a Sukoon), and because we can't start with a Saakin letter (as explained earlier), it is usually preceded by Hamzat-ulwasl (همزة الوصل).

Based on the letter that is immediately following Laam Atta'reef, we will either pronounce it or drop it as explained next:

i. Laam Qamariya (اللّام القمرية)

If the letter following Laam Atta'reef was one of the following letters, we pronounce Lam Atta'reef clearly (no hiding or merging). This is called **Izhar Qamari** (إظهار قمري) and Laam Atta'reef in this case will be called **Laam Qamariya** (اللّام القمرية). The letters are: (ا ب غ ح ج ك و خ ف ع ق ي م ه), which are collected in the phrase: " **ابغ حجك وخف عقيمه** "

The sign used on top of the Laam will tell us what type of Laam it is; this Sukoon sign (ْ◌) will be used on top of the Laam in case it is a Laam Qamariya (اللّام القمرية). Here are some examples:

(Al- muttahharoon) ٱلْمُطَهَّرُونَ

(Al-'Azeem) ٱلْعَظِيمِ

(Al-Qamar) ٱلْقَمَرُ

➔ **Note that the letters (ذ) and (ظ) can be found written in the transliteration as "th" or "z".**

ii. Laam Shamsiya (اللّام الشّمسيّة)

For the remaining letters of the Arabic Alphabet (other than those listed above with the Laam Qamariya), the Laam will be ***merged into the next letter***. This is called Idgham Shamsi (ادغام شمسي). Practically, the Laam will be dropped.

Laam Atta'reef in this case will be called Laam Shamsiya (اللّام الشّمسيّة), and it can be recognized by noticing it is left blank with no Sukoon sign (ْ◌), and the following letter has a Shadda (◌ّ). Here are some examples:

(Ash-shitaa') ٱلشِّتَآءِ

(Al-layl) ٱلَّيْلِ

(Ash-shams) ٱلشَّمْسِ

Noon Saakina & Other Saakin Letters

(النّون السّاكنة و الحروف السّاكنة الأخرى)

A Saakin letter (الحرف السّاكن) is a letter that has a Sukoon. The rules of Saakin letters are important in Tajweed, especially the rules of the **Noon (ن) Saakina**. Note that Saakin or Saakina means the same, but the first one is masculine, and the second one is feminine according to the Arabic grammar.

Saakin letters are marked in several ways in the Qur'anic text to indicate different Tajweed rules. ***So, you can tell what the Tajweed rule is by noticing the punctuation used on the Saakin letter, as will be explained next:***

i. Izhar (الإظهار)

Putting this Sukoon sign (ۡ) on top of any letter indicates it is a Saakin letter that should be pronounced clearly. The Tajweed rule, in this case, is Izhar, so there is no merging (i.e., Idgham) or hiding (i.e., Ikhfa'), as seen in the following examples:

(Min khairin) مِّنۡ خَيۡرٖ

(Wa yan'awna 'anhu) وَيَنۡـَٔوۡنَ عَنۡهُ

(Bi'abdihi) بِعَبۡدِهِۦ

(Qad sami'a) قَدۡ سَمِعَ

(Nadijat julooduhum) نَضِجَتۡ جُلُودُهُم

(Awa'athta) أَوَعَظۡتَ

(Wa khudtum) وَخُضۡتُمۡ

(Wa ith zaaghat) وَإِذۡ زَاغَتِ

وضع رأس خاء صغيرة بدون نقطة: (ح) فوق أي حرف يدل على سكون ذلك الحرف، وعلى أنه مُظهَر بحيث يقرعه اللسان، نحو: ﴿مِّنۡ خَيۡرٖ﴾، ﴿وَيَنۡـَٔوۡنَ عَنۡهُ﴾، ﴿بِعَبۡدِهِۦ﴾، ﴿قَدۡ سَمِعَ﴾، ﴿نَضِجَتۡ جُلُودُهُم﴾، ﴿أَوَعَظۡتَ﴾، ﴿وَخُضۡتُمۡ﴾، ﴿وَإِذۡ زَاغَتِ﴾.

Snippet from the original **"Convention of Dabt Signs (اصطلاحات ضبط المصحف)"**

ii. Full (Complete) Idgham (الإدغام الكامل)

If a Saakin letter (whether it is a Noon (ن) or any other letter) is left blank without any signs, and the next letter has Shadda (ّ), this indicates that the first letter should be merged into the next letter. The merging is complete as the sound of the first letter disappears, and the next letter is pronounced with Shadda. This is called Full (Complete) Idgham.

Note that Idgham of the Noon (ن) Saakina has two types; Full (Complete) Idgham and Incomplete Idgham, and the Dabt signs can tell us what type of Idgham it is. We will go over the Incomplete Idgham later, but here are examples of the Full Idgham:

- **Examples of the Full Idgham of the Noon (ن) Saakina:**

  مِن نَّارٍ (Minnar)

  مِّن مَّآءٍ (Mimmaa')

  مِن رَّبِّكَ (Mirrabbik)

  مِّن لَّدُنۡهُ (Milladunhu)

- **Examples of Full Idgham** **(for letters other than Noon (ن) Saakina):**

  - **"ت" merged into "د":**
    (Ujeebadda'watukumaa) أُجِيبَت دَّعۡوَتُكُمَا
  - **"ث" merged into "ذ":**
    (Yalhathaalika) يَلۡهَث ذَّٰلِكَ
  - **"ت" merged into "ط":**
    (Qaalattaa'ifatun) قَالَت طَّآئِفَةٌ
  - **"ه" merged into "ه":**
    (Wa mayyukrihhunna) وَمَن يُكۡرِههُّنَّ
  - **"ق" merged into "ك":**
    (Alam nakhlukkum) أَلَمۡ نَخۡلُقكُّم

> وتعرية الحرف من علامة السكون، مع تشديد الحرف التالي يدل على إدغام الأول في الثاني إدغاماً كاملاً، نحو: ﴿أُجِيبَت دَّعۡوَتُكُمَا﴾، ﴿يَلۡهَث ذَّٰلِكَ﴾، ﴿قَالَت طَّآئِفَةٌ﴾، ﴿وَمَن يُكۡرِههُّنَّ﴾، ﴿أَلَمۡ نَخۡلُقكُّم﴾.

Snippet from the original "**Convention of Dabt Signs** (اصطلاحات ضبط المصحف)"

iii. Ikhfa’ and Incomplete Idgham (الإخفاء و الإدغام الناقص)

If a Saakin letter is left blank without any sign, and there is no Shadda (◌ّ) on the next letter, the Tajweed rule then is ***either one of the following***:

- Ikhfa’ (الإخفاء)
- Incomplete Idgham (الإدغام الناقص)

In both Tajweed rules, we replace the letter Noon (ن) with Ghunna. Those Tajweed rules will be explained next.

a. Ikhfa' (الإخفاء)

When we do Ikhfa' on a letter, it is not pronounced clearly as in the case of Izhar, and it is not merged in the next letter as in the case of Idgham. When we apply Ikhfa' to a Noon Saakina (ن), we change it to a Ghunna (غنة), which is a nasal sound.

➔ ***Hint:** To pronounce the Ghunna (غنة) properly when doing Ikhfa', prepare the next letter with your mouth when you are pronouncing the Ghunna (غنة).*

The following examples are for the Ikhfa' of the Noon Saakina (ن) and the Meem Saakina (م), and we notice that they are left blank without any sign, and the next letter has no Shadda (ّ):

(Min tahtiha) مِن تَحۡتِهَا

(Min thamaratin) مِن ثَمَرَةٖ

(Inna Rabbahum bihim) إِنَّ رَبَّهُم بِهِمۡ

وتعريته مع عدم تشديد الحرف التالي: يدل على إخفاء الأول عند الثاني، فلا هو مظهر حتى يقرعه اللسان، ولا هُوَ مدغم حتى يقلب من جنس تاليه، نحو:

﴿مِن تَحۡتِهَا﴾، ﴿مِن ثَمَرَةٖ﴾، ﴿إِنَّ رَبَّهُم بِهِمۡ﴾

Snippet from the original "**Convention of Dabt Signs** (اصطلاحات ضبط المصحف)"

b. Incomplete Idgham (الإدغام الناقص)

In this type of Idgham, the first letter is merged into the second letter, but the merging is not complete, so the first letter keeps some of its attributes (like Ghunna, or the heaviness of the heavy letter).

As we mentioned above, Ikhfa' and Incomplete Idgham are marked the same way, so the first letter is left blank without any sign, and the next letter has no Shadda (ّ). Here are some examples:

مَن يَقُولُ (Mayyaqoolu)

مِن وَالٍ (Miwwaal)

مَا فَرَّطتُمْ (Ma farruttum)

بَسَطتَ (Basatta)

أو إدغامه فيه إدغاماً ناقصاً، نحو:
﴿ مَن يَقُولُ ﴾، ﴿ مِن وَالٍ ﴾، ﴿ مَافَرَّطتُمْ ﴾، ﴿ بَسَطتَ ﴾.

Snippet from the original "Convention of Dabt Signs (اصطلاحات ضبط المصحف)"

iv. Qalb (القلب)

Placing a small (م) above the Noon Saakina, instead of the Sukoon sign, indicates that the Noon Saakina is converted into Meem. This Meem should be pronounced with the proper length of the Ghunna. This Tajweed rule is called Qalb (القلب).

→ *Note: Qalb is sometimes referred to as Iqlab, but Qalb is the proper name.*

- **Examples:**

(Mimba'd) مِنۢ بَعۡدِ

(Mumbatha) مُّنۢبَثّٗا

ووضع ميم صغيرة (م) فوق النون الساكنة بدل السكون مع عدم تشديد الباء التالية، يدل على قلب النون ميماً، نحو: ﴿مِنۢ بَعۡدِ﴾، ﴿مُّنۢبَثّٗا﴾.

Snippet from the original **"Convention of Dabt Signs (اصطلاحات ضبط المصحف)"**

Summary of Noon Saakina

In the four rules above, we noticed that the Noon Saakina (ن) can either be:

- Pronounced as a clear Noon {**Izhar**}.
- Dropped (we drop the Noon totally) {**Complete Idgham**}.
- Pronounced as a Ghunna (we replace the noon with a Ghunna) {**Ikhfa' or Incomplete Idgham**}.
- Pronounced as a Meem (م) with Ghunna {**Qalb**}.

The signs used on the Noon Saakina (ن) provide us with hints on which rule to apply to it, as shown next:

- **Izhar:**

  Noon Saakina (ن) has this Sukoon sign (ْ):
  - Pronounce the Noon (ن) ***clearly*** with no Ghunna (غنة).

- **Complete Idgham:**

  Noon Saakina (ن) is left blank (with no Haraka (ِ , ُ , َ)) and the next letter has a Shadda (ّ):
  - Drop the Noon (ن) totally.

  Note that:

  - *If the next letter is either a (ن) or a (م), then you apply to that letter a Ghunna (غنة).*
  - *If the next letter is (ل) or (ر) then there is no Ghunna (غنة).*

- **Idgham Ikhfa' or Incomplete Idgham:**

  Noon Saakina (ن) was left blank (no Haraka (◌ِ , ◌ُ , ◌َ)) while there is no Shadda (◌ّ) on the next letter:

  - Replace the Noon Saakina (ن) with a Ghunna (غنّة).

- **Qalb**:
- Noon Saakina (ن) has a small Meem (م) on top:
  - Replace the Noon Saakina (ن) with Meem (م) and do a Ghunna (غنّة).

Summary Table for the Noon Saakina

The following table summarizes how to use the Tajweed signs to pronounce the Noon Saakina (ن) properly *even without knowing the Tajweed rule*:

If the Noon has	**A Sukoon (ۡ)**	**No Haraka (حركة) and the next letter has a Shadda (ّ)**	**No Haraka (حركة) and the next letter has no Shadda (ّ)**	**A small (م) on top**
Examples	مِنۡ أَهۡلِ	مِن رَّبِّكَ	مِن قَبۡلُ مَن يَقُولُ	مِنۢ بَعۡدِ
Pronounce as	Clear Noon	Drop the Noon totally	Ghunna (Replace the noon with Ghunna)	Meem (م) with Ghunna
Name of Tajweed Rule	Izhar (إظهار)	Complete Idgham (إدغام كامل)	Ikhfa' (إخفاء) or Incomplete Idgham (إدغام ناقص)	Qalb (قلب)

Table (1)

Tanween Rules (أحكام التنوين)

Tanween (ٍ , ٌ , ً) is composed of a pair of Harakat (plural of Haraka in Arabic). The Haraka can be either a Fat'ha (َ), a Dumma (ُ), or a Kasra (ِ). Tanween can be found on the last letter of certain words according to Arabic grammar.

➔ *Tanween is written in different ways in the Qur'anic text, and each way gives a hint on which Tajweed rule to apply (Izhar, Idgham, Ikhfa', or Qalb). The different ways of writing the Tanween will be explained next.*

i. Izhar (الإظهار)

Displaying the Tanween as (ـً ـٌ ـٍ) indicates the Tajweed rule is Izhar, which means that the Tanween should be pronounced clearly (as a Noon (ن) sound). Here are some examples:

(Wala sharaaban illa) وَلَا شَرَابًا ﴿٢٤﴾ إِلَّا

(Samee'un 'Aleem) سَمِيعٌ عَلِيمٌ

(Wa likulli qawmin haad) وَلِكُلِّ قَوْمٍ هَادٍ

تركيب الحركتين فتحتين أوضمتين أوكسرتين، هكذا (ـً ـٌ ـٍ) يدل على إظهار التنوين ، نحو:
﴿ وَلَا شَرَابًا ﴿٢٤﴾ إِلَّا ﴾ ، ﴿ سَمِيعٌ عَلِيمٌ ﴾ ﴿ وَلِكُلِّ قَوْمٍ هَادٍ ﴾ .

Snippet from the original **"Convention of Dabt Signs (اصطلاحات ضبط المصحف)"**

ii. Full (Complete) Idgham (الإدغام الكامل)

Displaying the Tanween as (ـً ـٌ ـٍ) while the next letter has a Shadda (ّ) indicates that the Tajweed rule is Full (Complete) Idgham, which means that the Tanween sound disappears completely, and we pronounce the next letter with Shadda. Here are some examples:

(Ghafoorar Raheema) غَفُورًا رَّحِيمًا

(Khushubum musannadah) خُشُبٌ مُّسَنَّدَةٌ

(Yawma 'ithin naa'imah) يَوْمَئِذٍ نَّاعِمَةٌ

وتتابُعُها هكذا (ـً ـٌ ـٍ): مع تشديد التالي، يدُل على الإدغام الكامل، نحو: ﴿غَفُورًا رَّحِيمًا﴾ ﴿خُشُبٌ مُّسَنَّدَةٌ﴾ ﴿يَوْمَئِذٍ نَّاعِمَةٌ﴾.

Snippet from the original **"Convention of Dabt Signs (اصطلاحات ضبط المصحف)"**

iii. Ikhfa' and Incomplete Idgham (الإخفاء و الإدغام الناقص)

Displaying the Tanween as (ـً ـٌ ـٍ) while there is no Shadda (ّ◌) on the next letter, indicates that the Tajweed rule is ***either one of the following two cases***:

- Ikhfa' (الإخفاء)
- Incomplete Idgham (الإدغام الناقص)

In both Tajweed rules, we replace the Noon sound of the Tanween with Ghunna. Those Tajweed rules will be explained next.

i. Ikhfa' (الإخفاء)

As mentioned earlier, when we do Ikhfa' on a letter, it is not pronounced clearly as in the case of Izhar, and it is not merged in the next letter as in the case of Idgham.

When we apply Ikhfa' to a Tanween, we change it to a Ghunna (غنّة), which is a nasal sound.

The Tanween, in the case of Ikhfa', will be displayed as shown in the following examples:

(Siraa'an thalik) سِرَاعًا ذَٰلِكَ

(Shihaabon thaqib) شِهَابٌ ثَاقِبٌ

(Mutaa'in thamma 'ameen) مُّطَاعٍ ثَمَّ أَمِينٍ

وتتابُعُها مع عدم التشديد : يدُلّ على الإخفاء، نحو : ﴿ سِرَاعًا ذَٰلِكَ ﴾ ، ﴿ شِهَابٌ ثَاقِبٌ ﴾ ، ﴿ مُّطَاعٍ ثَمَّ أَمِينٍ ﴾ .

Snippet from the original **"Convention of Dabt Signs (اصطلاحات ضبط المصحف)"**

ii. Incomplete Idgham (الإدغام الناقص)

When we apply Incomplete Idgham to a Tanween, the Tanween is merged into the next letter, but the merging is not complete, which means that the Ghunna sound remains when we pronounce the next letter.

In the case of Incomplete Idgham, the Tanween will be displayed in the same way as in Ikhfa', as shown in the following examples:

(Raheemuw Wadood) رَحِيمٌ وَدُودٌ

(Wujoohuy yawma 'ithin) وُجُوهٌ يَوْمَئِذٍ

أو الإدغام الناقص نحو: ﴿ رَحِيمٌ وَدُودٌ ﴾ ، ﴿ وُجُوهٌ يَوْمَئِذٍ ﴾ .

Snippet from the original **"Convention of Dabt Signs (اصطلاحات ضبط المصحف)"**

→ *Note that in the cases of Full (Complete) Idgham, Ikhfa', or Incomplete Idgham, the Fat'ha Tanween (تنوين الفتح) can be either written* as (ً) or (ً). *(The position of the upper Fat'ha is to the right of the lower Fat'ha in one case, and to the left of the lower Fat'ha in the other case).*

iii. Qalb (القلب)

If the second Haraka of the Tanween is replaced with a small Meem (م), the Tajweed rule of Qalb should be applied to the Tanween. Applying Qalb to the Tanween means that the Noon sound of the Tanween is converted into the sound of Meem (م). This Meem should be pronounced with the proper length of the Ghunna. Here are some examples:

(Jazaa'am bima kaanoo) جَزَآءَۢ بِمَا كَانُواْ

(Aleemum bithatissudoor) عَلِيمُۢ بِذَاتِ ٱلصُّدُورِ

(Kiraamim bararah) كِرَامِۭ بَرَرَةٖ

ووضع ميم صغيرة (م) بدل الحركة الثانية من التنوين مع عدم تشديد الباء التالية، يدل على قلب التنوين ميماً، نحو: ﴿ جَزَآءَۢ بِمَا كَانُواْ ﴾، ﴿ عَلِيمُۢ بِذَاتِ ٱلصُّدُورِ ﴾، ﴿ كِرَامِۭ بَرَرَةٖ ﴾.

Snippet from the original **"Convention of Dabt Signs (اصطلاحات ضبط المصحف)"**

Summary of Tanween Rules

In the four rules above, we noticed that the Tanween sound (similar to the Noon Saakina), can either be:

- Pronounced as a clear Noon {**<u>Izhar</u>**}.
- Dropped (we drop the Tanween totally) {**<u>Complete Idgham</u>**}.
- Pronounced as a Ghunna (we replace the Tanween with a Ghunna) {**<u>Ikhfa' or Incomplete Idgham</u>**}.
- Pronounced as a Meem (م) with Ghunna {**<u>Qalb</u>**}.

The Tanween is written in different ways based on which Tajweed rule to apply; therefore, we can tell what rule to apply by noticing how the Tanween is written as shown next:

- Tanween is written as (ـٍ ـٌ ـً):
  - ➢ Pronounce as a clear Noon (ن) with no Ghunna (غنة).
- Tanween is written as (ـٍ ـٌ ـً) and the next letter has a Shadda (ـّ):
  - ➢ Skip the Tanween (no (ن) sound) and go to the next letter.

Note that:

- *If the next letter is either a (ن) or a (م), then you apply to that letter a Ghunna (غنة).*
- *If the next letter is either a (ل) or a (ر) then there is no Ghunna (غنة).*

- Tanween is written as (ٍ ٌ ً) and there is no Shadda (ّ) on the next letter:
    - ➢ Replace the Tanween sound with a Ghunna (غنّة).

- The second Haraka of the Tanween is changed into a small Meem (م):
    - ➢ Replace the Noon sound of the Tanween with a Meem sound and do a Ghunna (غنّة).

Summary Table for Tanween

The following table summarizes how to use the Tajweed signs to pronounce the Tanween properly *even without knowing the Tajweed rule:*

Tanween is written as	(ٍ ٌ ً)	(ٍ ٌ ً) and the next letter has a Shadda (ّ)	(ٍ ٌ ً) and the next letter has no Shadda (ّ)	The second Haraka of the Tanween is replaced with a small Meem (م)
Examples	سَمِيعٌ عَلِيمٌ	صِرَٰطٍ مُّسْتَقِيمٍ	شِهَابٌ ثَاقِبٌ نُورًا وَهُدًى	كِرَامٍۭ بَرَرَةٍ
Pronounce as	Clear Noon	Drop Tanween totally	Ghunna	Meem (م) with Ghunna
Name of Tajweed Rule	Izhar (إظهار)	Complete Idgham (إدغام كامل)	Ikhfa' (إخفاء) or Incomplete Idgham (إدغام ناقص)	Qalb (قلب)

Table (2)

Madd (المدّ)

Madd means lengthening or stretching, and it applies to the long vowel letters (ي , و , ا), which are called the ***letters of Madd (or Madd letters)***. The length we apply to those letters is measured in Haraka. The timing of a Haraka (or one count) is the time it takes to pronounce any letter with a Haraka (ـِ , ـُ , ـَ). So, a Fat'ha (ـَ), a Dumma (ـُ), or a Kasra (ـِ) is a Haraka. The same word (Haraka) is also used to measure the time to pronounce a letter with a Haraka (ـِ , ـُ , ـَ).

Two-Haraka timing (or 2 counts) is the time to pronounce a Madd letter (ي , و , ا) in its natural (original) length. Placing the Madd sign *(~)* above the Madd letters indicates that it will need to be lengthened (stretched) more than the original length.

➔ *Madd letters can be stretched between 2 to 6 Harakat depending on the type of Madd. Certain types of Madd can have a range of lengths (for example, 4-6 Harakat), but for the sake of simplicity, we are limiting our choice of lengths in this book to fixed lengths, which is an acceptable and authentic choice.*

Next, we will learn how to apply a proper length to the Madd letters simply by using the text and the signs used on the Madd letter, ***even if we don't know the types of the Madd.***

The length of the Madd letters in this book will be either 2, 4, or 6 Counts (Harakat) as explained next:

i. Two-Counts Madd

The original length of the Madd letters is 2 counts, which is the time it takes to pronounce those letters in their natural length without additional stretching.

No Madd sign (~) is placed on the Madd letter when it is in the natural length.

- **Examples:**
  - Madd of the Alif (ا) in:
    (Alhaakumut takaathur) أَلْهَىٰكُمُ ٱلتَّكَاثُرُ
  - Madd of the Waw (و) in:
    (Qul a'ootho bi Rabbil falaq) قُلْ أَعُوذُ بِرَبِّ ٱلْفَلَقِ
  - Madd of the Yaa (ي) in:
    (Fi jeediha hablum mim masad) فِي جِيدِهَا حَبْلٌ مِّن مَّسَدٍ

➔ *Note: Madd letters will need to be stretched more than the natural length if and only if they are followed by either a Hamza or a Sukoon.*

ii. Four-Counts Madd

We will apply the 4-count length to the following two categories of Madd:

a) Madd Due to Hamza (ء)

If the Madd sign (~) is placed on top of a Madd letter, and the next letter is a Hamza (ء), then you stretch the Madd letter to 4 counts.

- Note that there are multiple types of Madd caused by the Hamza (ء), and the range of length for them varies between 2 to 6 counts. Our choice is to apply 4 counts to any Madd caused by a Hamza (ء), which is a strong and authentic choice.

Examples:

- Alif (ا) followed by a Hamza (ء):
  (Itha <u>jaa</u>'a nasrullaahi wal fat'h) إِذَا جَآءَ نَصۡرُ ٱللَّهِ وَٱلۡفَتۡحُ
- Waw (و) followed by a Hamza (ء):
  (Qaal<u>oo</u> 'innaa tataiyarnaa bikum) قَالُوٓاْ إِنَّا تَطَيَّرۡنَا بِكُمۡ
- Ya (ي) followed by a Hamza (ء):
  (Am yaj'alu lahoo Rabb<u>ee</u> amada) أَمۡ يَجۡعَلُ لَهُۥ رَبِّيٓ أَمَدًا

→Note that the letters corresponding to the Madd letters have been underlined in the transliteration.

b) Madd Due to Temporary Sukoon

As mentioned above, one of the two causes of Madd (to stretch the Madd letter more than 2 counts) is having a Sukoon on the next letter (that follows the Madd letter).

The Sukoon on letters can be either original or temporary (unoriginal). Madd due to the original Sukoon will be discussed later in the "6-Counts Madd" section. The following two types of Madd are caused by having a temporary (unoriginal) Sukoon after the Madd letter:

1. Madd 'Arid Lissukoon (المد العارض للسكون)
2. Madd Leen (مد اللّين)

➔ ***Note: In Arabic, when you stop on a word, the last letter becomes Saakin (ساكن), which means it gets a Sukoon. If the second-to-last letter happens to be a Madd letter or a Leen letter, then we apply Madd 'Arid Lissukoon (المد العارض للسكون) or Madd Leen (مد اللّين) as explained below.***

Those two types of Madd do not have the Madd sign (~), but we can recognize them when we understand their rules, so here is a quick review of them:

1. **Madd 'Arid Lissukoon (المد العارض للسكون):**

If the second-to-last letter (before we stop at the end of the Aya, or even in the middle of the Aya), happens to be a Madd letter (ا , و ,ي), we can stretch it to 2, 4, or 6 counts. Our choice in this book is to limit this type of Madd to 4 counts (which is an acceptable and authentic choice).

Here are some examples:

- Stretching the (ي) in:
  (Alhamdu lillahi Rubil 'aalameen) ٱلْحَمْدُ لِلَّهِ رَبِّ ٱلْعَٰلَمِينَ
- Stretching the (و) in:
  (Qul yaa 'ayyuhal kaafiroon) قُلْ يَٰٓأَيُّهَا ٱلْكَٰفِرُونَ

Note that the letters corresponding to the Madd letters have been underlined in the transliteration.

2. Madd Leen (مد اللّين)

This Madd is similar to Madd 'Arid Lissukoon, but it is applied to the Leen letters.

Leen letter is either (و or ي) that has a Sukoon *while the preceding letter has a Fat'ha (ـَ).*

If the second-to-last letter (before we stop at the end of the Aya, or in the middle of the Aya), happens to be a Leen letter, we can stretch it to 2, 4, or 6 counts. Our choice is to limit this type of Madd also to 4 counts (which is totally acceptable). Here are examples:

- Stretching the (ي):

  (Haathal bayt) هَٰذَا ٱلْبَيْتِ

- Stretching the (و):

  (Min khawf) مِّنْ خَوْفٍ

Note that the letters corresponding to the Leen letters have been underlined in the transliteration.

Both Madd Leen and Madd 'Arid Lissukoon are applied to the

second-to-last letter when we pause or stop reading and can be stretched to the same count.

➔ *We will be choosing a length of 4 counts for those two types of Madd, and since they are caused by a temporary Sukoon, we will be referring to them as "Temporary Sukoon" Madd types. Technically, it is better to call them "Due-to-Temporary Sukoon" Mad, but for simplicity, we will call them "Temporary Sukoon" Madd types.*

iii. Six-Counts Madd

The only type of Madd that we will stretch to 6 counts is Madd Lazim. In Madd Lazim, we stretch the Madd letter when it is followed by a Shadda (ّ) or a Sukoon (ْ). It does not have a range of length; we stretch it to a fixed length of 6 counts.

Madd Lazim can be recognized by noticing the Madd sign (~) on top of the Madd letter while the next letter has either a Shadda (ّ) or a Sukoon (ْ), like:

- Madd letter followed by Shadda (ّ):

  (Addaalleen) ٱلضَّآلِّينَ

- Madd letter followed by a Sukoon (ْ):

  (Aal'aana) ءَآلْـَٔنَ

Note that:

- If the Madd Lazim is due a Shadda (ّ) following the Madd letter, it will be called Madd Lazim Muthaqqal (مد لازم مثقّل).
- If the Madd Lazim is due a Sukoon (ْ) following the Madd letter, it will be called Madd Lazim Mukhaffaf (مد لازم مخفّف).

Madd Lazim is also found in the "Huroof Muqatta'a" (لحروف المقطّعة), which are the letters found at the beginning of some Suras of the Qur'an. Here are some examples:

(Alif Laam Raa) الٓر

(Haa Meem) حمٓ

(Kaaf Haa Yaa 'Ain Saad) كٓهيعٓصٓ

Note that the Shadda (ّ) and the Sukoon (ْ) are not written in the "Huroof Muqatta'a" (الحروف المقطّعة).

➔ *Hint: A common thing between all types of the Madd Lazim is that the Madd letter has a Madd sign (~) while the next letter is not a Hamza (ء). This is an easy way to know when to apply the 6-counts Madd. So, anytime you see the Madd sign (~) while the next letter is not a Hamza (ء) you can tell that this is a Madd Lazim, and it should be stretched to 6 counts.*

Summary of Madd

The following summary shows how to do the Madd correctly ***even without knowing the types of Madd***. Note that the length of the Madd letters varies depending on the Tajweed rules, but following this summary allows you to do the Madd properly with an acceptable Madd length.

- **Two Counts:** The natural length of the Madd letters (ي , و , ا). Applies to the Madd letters when there is no Madd sign and when the Temporary Sukoon Madd does not apply.
- **Four Counts:** Applies to:
  - Madd letters with a Madd sign (~) followed by a Hamza (ء).
  - Temporary Sukoon Madd.
- **Six Counts:** Applies to Madd letters with a Madd sign (~) while the following letter is **<u>not</u>** a Hamza (ء).

Summary Table for Madd

The following table includes a summary of the Dabt signs for the Madd:

Length of Madd Letter	6 Counts	4 Counts	2 Counts
Examples	ٱلضَّآلِّينَ	مَآ أَعۡبُدُ ٱلۡحَمۡدُ لِلَّهِ رَبِّ ٱلۡعَٰلَمِينَ هَٰذَا ٱلۡبَيۡتِ	ٱلصِّرَٰطَ
How to Recognize	Madd letter: - Has a Madd sign (~). And - Is not followed by a Hamza (ء).	- Madd letter has a Madd sign (~), and the next letter is a Hamza (ء). Or - The Temporary Sukoon Madd.	- No Madd sign (~). And - It is not the Temporary Sukoon Madd.

Table (3)

Additional examples on Madd

Here are some additional examples of Madd. Note that anytime you see the Madd sign (~) you will need to stretch the Madd letter more than the original length. More about the different Madd types can be found in the Tajweed books.

- **6 Counts Madd:**

(Alif Laam Meem) الٓمٓ

(Attaammatu) ٱلطَّآمَّةُ

- **4 Counts Madd:**

(Quroo'in) قُرُوٓءٖ

(See'a bihim) سِيٓءَ بِهِمۡ

(Shufa'aa'a) شُفَعَٰٓؤُاْ

(Ta'weeluhoo illallaah) تَأۡوِيلَهُۥٓ إِلَّا ٱللَّهُ

(laa yastahyee ay yadriba) لَا يَسۡتَحۡيِۦٓ أَن يَضۡرِبَ

بِمَآ أُنزِلَ (Bimaa unzila)

قُوٓاْ أَنفُسَكُمۡ (Qoo anfusakum)

ووضع هذه العلامة (~) فوق الحرف يدل على مده مدا زائداً على المد الأصلي الطبيعي،نحو: ﴿ الٓمٓ ﴾، ﴿ ٱلطَّآمَّةُ ﴾، ﴿قُرُوٓءٍ﴾، ﴿ سِيٓـَٔ بِهِمۡ ﴾، ﴿ شُفَعَٰٓؤُاْ ﴾، ﴿ تَأۡوِيلَهُۥٓ إِلَّا ٱللَّهُ ﴾، ﴿ لَا يَسۡتَحۡيِۦٓ أَن يَضۡرِبَ ﴾، ﴿ بِمَآ أُنزِلَ ﴾، ﴿ قُوٓاْ أَنفُسَكُمۡ ﴾، على تفصيل يعلم من فن التجويد.

Snippet from the original "**Convention of Dabt Signs** (اصطلاحات ضبط المصحف)"

Small-size Letters (الحروف الصغيرة)

The small-size letters are used in the Qur'anic text in the following ways:

i. **Addition:** Small-size letters ***added*** to the Qur'anic text to indicate that you should pronounce the small-size letter even though it is not written in the original text, as seen in the examples below:

- **Small Alif (ا):**
  (Thaalikal Kitaabu) ذَٰلِكَ ٱلْكِتَٰبُ

- **Small Alif (ا) and small Waw (و):**
  (Yaa Daawoodu) يَٰدَاوُۥدُ

- **Small Waw (و):**
  (Yalwoona alsinatahum) يَلْوُۥنَ أَلْسِنَتَهُم

- **Small Yaa (ے):**
  (Yuhyee wa yumeetu) يُحْيِۦ وَيُمِيتُ

  (Anta waliyyi fiddunya walaakhirati) أَنتَ وَلِيِّۦ فِي ٱلدُّنْيَا وَٱلْأٓخِرَةِ

  (Inna waliyyiyallahu) إِنَّ وَلِـِّۧيَ ٱللَّهُ

  (Lilhawaariyyeena) لِلْحَوَارِيِّـۧنَ

(Eelafihim rihlatashitaa'i wassaif) إِۦلَٰفِهِمْ رِحْلَةَ ٱلشِّتَآءِ وَٱلصَّيْفِ

(Bihee Baseera) بِهِۦ بَصِيرًا

(Biyameenihi fa yaqool) بِيَمِينِهِۦ فَيَقُولُ

- **Small Noon (ۨ):**

(Wa kathaalika nunjil mu'mineen) وَكَذَٰلِكَ نُۨجِي ٱلْمُؤْمِنِينَ

والحروف الصغيرة، تدل على أعيان الحروف المتروكة في المصاحف العثمانية مع وجوب النطق بها، نحو:
﴿ ذَٰلِكَ ٱلْكِتَٰبُ ﴾، ﴿ يَٰدَاوُۥدُ ﴾، ﴿ يَلْوُۥنَ أَلْسِنَتَهُم ﴾،
﴿ يُحْيِۦ وَيُمِيتُ ﴾، ﴿ أَنتَ وَلِيِّۦ فِي ٱلدُّنْيَا وَٱلْأَخِرَةِ ﴾،
﴿ إِنَّ وَلِـِّۧيَ ٱللَّهُ ﴾، ﴿ لِلْحَوَارِيِّۧنَ ﴾، ﴿ إِۦلَٰفِهِمْ رِحْلَةَ ٱلشِّتَآءِ وَٱلصَّيْفِ ﴾،
﴿ بِهِۦ بَصِيرًا ﴾، ﴿ بِيَمِينِهِۦ فَيَقُولُ ﴾، ﴿ وَكَذَٰلِكَ نُۨجِي ٱلْمُؤْمِنِينَ ﴾.

Snippet from the original **"Convention of Dabt Signs (اصطلاحات ضبط المصحف)"**

➔ *Note that the original Qur'anic text cannot be changed from the way it was written at the time of the prophet Muhammad (peace be upon him). These small letters are used for sounds that we pronounce but were not part of the original text. They were added to specific words that were written slightly differently from how they appear in the standard Arabic text."*

ii. **Substitution:** Small-size letters can also be placed ***above*** certain letters to indicate that you should pronounce the small-size letter ***instead of*** the original letter that is written in the text, as seen below:

- **Small Alif (ٰ):**

(Assalaah) ٱلصَّلَوٰةَ

(Kamishkaah) كَمِشْكَوٰةٍ

(Arribaa) ٱلرِّبَوٰاْ

(Wa ithistasqaa Musaa) وَإِذِ ٱسْتَسْقَىٰ مُوسَىٰ

(Laqad ra'aa) لَقَدْ رَأَىٰ

- **Small Seen** (س):

(Wallahu yaqbidu wayabsut) وَٱللَّهُ يَقْبِضُ وَيَبْصُۜطُ

وإن كان الحرف المتروك، له بدل في الكتابة الأصلية
عُوِّل في النطق على الحرف المُلْحَق لا على البدل، نحو:
﴿ٱلصَّلَوٰةِ﴾، ﴿كَمِشْكَوٰةٍ﴾، ﴿ٱلرِّبَوٰاْ﴾، ﴿وَإِذِ ٱسْتَسْقَىٰ مُوسَىٰ﴾،
﴿لَقَدْ رَأَىٰ﴾ ونحو: ﴿وَٱللَّهُ يَقْبِضُ وَيَبْصُۜطُ﴾.

Snippet from the original **"Convention of Dabt Signs (اصطلاحات ضبط المصحف)"**

iii. **Less common (but acceptable):** Placing a small (س) *under* the letter (ص) indicates that reading the word with (ص) is more common. So, while reading the word with (س) is less common than reading it with (ص), it is still acceptable as it has also been narrated that way.

- **Example:**

  (Almusaitiroon) ٱلۡمُصَۣيۡطِرُونَ

فإن وضعت السين تحت الصاد دلَّت على النطق بالصاد،
نحو: ﴿ ٱلۡمُصَۣيۡطِرُونَ ﴾.

Snippet from the original "*Convention of Dabt Signs* (اصطلاحات ضبط المصحف)"

Large Dot (•)

The large dot can be used to indicate one of the following rules:

i. Imala (الإمالة)

Placing a large dot under the letter (ر) in the word shown below indicates that "Imala" (إمالة) should be applied to the letter (ا) following the letter (ر). Specifically, this Imala is called Imala Kubra (إمالة كبرى). It is done by pronouncing the (ا) in a way between its original sound and the sound of the (ي).

(Bismillahi majraiha) بِسْمِ ٱللَّهِ مَجْرِىٰهَا [4]

→ Note: Some prints of the Qur'anic text use a small diamond shape to mark the Imala as seen below:

(Bismillahi majraiha بِسۡمِ ٱللَّهِ مَجۡرِىٰهَا

ووضع النقطة تحت الراء في قوله تعالى:
﴿ بِسۡمِ ٱللَّهِ مَجۡرِىٰهَا ﴾ يدل على إمالة الألف الذي
بعد الراء نحو الياء، إمالة كبرى.

Snippet from the original **"Convention of Dabt Signs (اصطلاحات ضبط المصحف)"**

[4] Surat 11 (Hud): Ayah 41.

**Note that the Aya number and the Sura are not mentioned for all the examples provided in the book. They are only mentioned in the footnotes for certain examples that have unique words.

ii. Ishmaam (الإشمام)

Placing a large dot above the end of the letter (م) before the Noon Mushaddada (نّ) in the word (تَأْمَنَّا) as shown below, indicates that Ishmam should be applied to the Noon Saakina.

Remember that Noon Mushaddada (نّ) (or Noon with Shadda (ّ)) is composed of two Noon letters, and the first one of them is a Noon Saakina.

Ishmam is done by rounding the lips as we do when pronouncing the Dumma (ُ), but no actual Dumma is pronounced (just the lips are rounded without the sound of Dumma).

(Malaka la ta'manna) مَا لَكَ لَا تَأْمَنَّا [5]

➔ Note: Some prints use a small diamond shape to mark the Ishmaam instead of the large dot as seen below:

(Malaka la ta'manna) مَا لَكَ لَا تَأْمَنَّا

---

[5] Surat 12 (Yousuf): Aya 11

ووضع النقطة المذكورة فوق آخر الميم قبيل النون المشددة من قوله تعالى: ﴿ مَالَكَ لَا تَأْمَنَّا ﴾، يدل على الإشمام وهو ضم الشفتين كمن يريد النطق بضمة، إشارة إلى أن الحركة المحذوفة ضمة من غير أن يظهر لذلك أثر في النطق.

Snippet from the original **"Convention of Dabt Signs (اصطلاحات ضبط المصحف)"**

Note that, for this word (تَأۡمَ۫نَّا), there is another acceptable way of reading; instead of applying Ishmam, you can apply Ikhtilas (إختلاس) (which is sometimes called Rawm (الرَّوم)).

As a quick note about Ikhtilas, the word (تَأۡمَ۫نَّا) has originally a Dumma on the first Noon. To do Ikhtilas, you pronounce the first Noon with a quick and short Dumma while lowering your voice. More details can be found in advanced Tajweed books.

iii. Tas-heel Al-Hamza (تسهيل الهمزة)

Placing the large dot on the second Hamza of the word shown below indicates Tas-heel Al-Hamza should be applied. This means the Hamza is pronounced in a way between the original sound of the Hamza (ء) and the sound of the Alif (ا).

- When you pronounce the Hamza (ء) you close your throat, while when you pronounce the Alif (ا) your throat is open. With Tas-heel Al-Hamza (Tas-heel of the Hamza) we keep our throat in between being totally closed and wide open, as in the following word:

(A'a'jamiyyun) ءَاعْجَمِيٌّ [6]

ووضع نقطة مدورة مسدودة الوسط فوق الهمزة الثانية من قوله تعالى ﴿ءَاعْجَمِيٌّ﴾، يدل على تسهيلها بين بين، أي بين الهمزة والألف.

Snippet from the original "**Convention of Dabt Signs (اصطلاحات ضبط المصحف)**"

[6] Surat 41 (Fussilat): Aya 44

Ta' Maftooha and Ta' Marboota (التاء المفتوحة و التاء المربوطة)

When you stop on a Ta' Maftooha (ت) you pronounce it normally as a Ta' with Sukoon, but when you stop on a Ta' Marboota (ة or ـة) you change it to a Ha' (هـ) with Sukoon.

- **Examples:**
  - **Ta' Maftooha (ت):**

    (Rahmat) رَحۡمَتِ

    (Ni'mat) نِعۡمَتَ

    (Imra'at) ٱمۡرَأَتُ

  - **Ta' Marboota (ة or ـة):**

    (Kalimatin sawaa') كَلِمَةٖ سَوَآءِۭ

    (Al-Ghaashiyah) ٱلۡغَٰشِيَةِ

    (Al-bayyinah") ٱلۡبَيِّنَةُ

وكل تاء رُسمت مفتوحة مثل (رحمت) و(نعمت) و(امرأت) فإن حفصاً يقف عليها بالتاء المفتوحة. فإذا رسمت بالتاء المربوطة مثل (كلمةٍ سواء) فالجميع يقفون عليها بالهاء.

Snippet from the original "**Convention of Dabt Signs** (اصطلاحات ضبط المصحف)"

End-of-Aya Sign (علامة نهاية الآية)

This round sign (۝١) marks the end of the Aya, and the number inside it is the number of the Aya. This sign is always placed at the **end** of the Aya, *so it belongs to the Aya before the sign. not the next Aya.*

- **Example:**

إِنَّآ أَعۡطَيۡنَٰكَ ٱلۡكَوۡثَرَ ۝١ فَصَلِّ لِرَبِّكَ وَٱنۡحَرۡ

(Inna a'taynakal Kawthar ۝١ Fasalli liRabbika wanhar)

والدائرة المحلاة التي في جوفها رقم: تدل بهيئتها على انتهاء الآية، ورقمها يدل على رقم تلك الآية في السورة، نحو:
﴿ إِنَّآ أَعۡطَيۡنَٰكَ ٱلۡكَوۡثَرَ ۝١ فَصَلِّ لِرَبِّكَ وَٱنۡحَرۡ ﴾، ولا يجوز وضعها قبل الآية البتة، فلذلك لا توجد في بداية الآية وتوجد في آخرها.

Snippet from the original "**Convention of Dabt Signs** (اصطلاحات ضبط المصحف)"

Sujood-Attilawa Marks (علامات سجود التلاوة)

Sujood Attilawa or prostration of recitation is making a Sujood (prostration) after reciting certain Ayat that mention Sujood.

Sujood Attilawa is marked by a horizontal line above the word that mention the Sujood, and by this sign (۩) which marks when to stop the recitation and do the Sujood (you keep on reading until that sign, then you make the Sujood).

Here is an example:

وَلِلَّهِ يَسْجُدُ مَا فِي ٱلسَّمَٰوَٰتِ وَمَا فِي ٱلْأَرْضِ مِن دَآبَّةٍ
وَٱلْمَلَٰٓئِكَةُ وَهُمْ لَا يَسْتَكْبِرُونَ ﴿٤٩﴾ يَخَافُونَ رَبَّهُم مِّن فَوْقِهِمْ
وَيَفْعَلُونَ مَا يُؤْمَرُونَ ۩ ﴿٥٠﴾

(Walillahi yasjudu ma fissamaawaati wama fil Ardi min daabatin wal malaa'ikatu wahum laa yastakbiroon (49) yakhaafoona Rubbahum min fawkihim wayaf'aloona maa yu'maroon (50)).

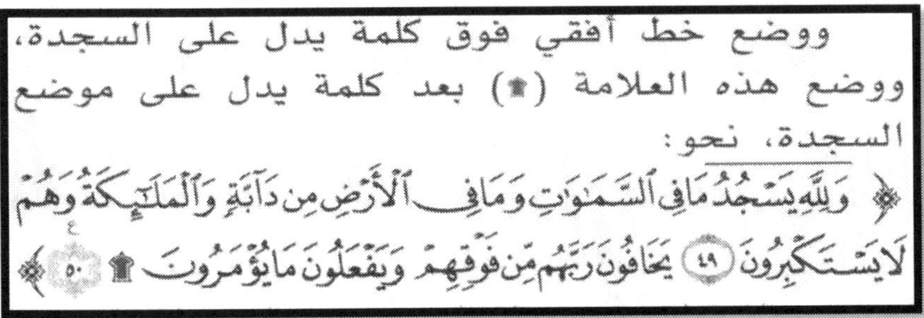

ووضع خط أفقي فوق كلمة يدل على السجدة،
ووضع هذه العلامة (۩) بعد كلمة يدل على موضع السجدة، نحو:
﴿ وَلِلَّهِ يَسْجُدُ مَا فِي ٱلسَّمَٰوَٰتِ وَمَا فِي ٱلْأَرْضِ مِن دَآبَّةٍ وَٱلْمَلَٰٓئِكَةُ وَهُمْ
لَا يَسْتَكْبِرُونَ ﴿٤٩﴾ يَخَافُونَ رَبَّهُم مِّن فَوْقِهِمْ وَيَفْعَلُونَ مَا يُؤْمَرُونَ ۩ ﴿٥٠﴾ ﴾

Snippet from the original **"Convention of Dabt Signs (اصطلاحات ضبط المصحف)"**

Marks for Beginning of Juz' or Hizb (علامة بداية الجزء أو الحزب)

This sign (۞) is used to mark the beginning of a Juz', the beginning of a Hizb (which is half a Juz'), the beginning of half a Hizb, or the beginning of a quarter of a Hizb.

- **Example:**

فَأَلْقِيَاهُ فِي ٱلْعَذَابِ ٱلشَّدِيدِ ﴿٢٦﴾ ۞ قَالَ قَرِينُهُۥ رَبَّنَا مَآ أَطْغَيْتُهُۥ

(Fa alqiyaahu fil 'athabishadeed (26) ۞ Qaala qareenuhoo Rabbana maa atghaytuhu)

➔ Note that this sign can be found as (۞) , (❋), or similar. Also note that it is not displayed at the beginning of the first Juz' of the Qur'an.

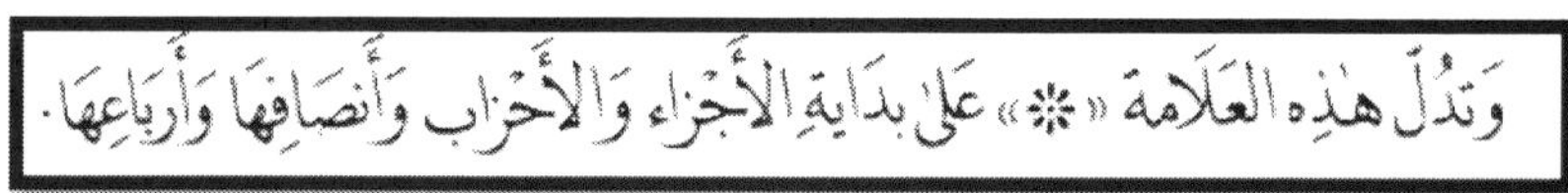

وَتَدُلّ هَٰذِهِ الْعَلَامَة «❋» عَلَىٰ بِدَايَةِ الْأَجْزَاءِ وَالْأَحْزَابِ وَأَنْصَافِهَا وَأَرْبَاعِهَا.

Snippet from the original "**Convention of Dabt Signs** (اصطلاحات ضبط المصحف)"

Stopping Signs (علامات الوقف)

Stopping signs in the Qur'anic text mark where to stop your recitation. Note that stopping means you stop for a moment and then resume recitation.

The following signs are used to mark the different types of stops:

- (مـ) - Marks a **compulsory stop** (الوقف اللازم):
  - ➢ The reciter should stop.
  - Example:

إِنَّمَا يَسْتَجِيبُ ٱلَّذِينَ يَسْمَعُونَ ۘ وَٱلْمَوْتَىٰ يَبْعَثُهُمُ ٱللَّهُ

- (لا) - Marks a **prohibited stop** (الوقف الممنوع):
  - ➢ Stopping is not allowed.
  - Example:

ٱلَّذِينَ تَتَوَفَّىٰهُمُ ٱلْمَلَٰٓئِكَةُ طَيِّبِينَ ۙ يَقُولُونَ سَلَٰمٌ عَلَيْكُمُ

- (ج) - Marks a **permissible stop** (الوقف الجائز):

  - ➢ Stopping is allowed. **It is your choice to stop or not.**

  - **Example:**

فَٱصۡفَحۡ عَنۡهُمۡ وَقُلۡ سَلَٰمٞۚ فَسَوۡفَ يَعۡلَمُونَ

- (صلى) - Marks a **permissible stop** while it *is preferred to continue* (الوقف الجائز مع كون الوصل أولى):

  - ➢ It is your choice to stop or continue, but it is preferred to continue.

  - **Example:**

أُوْلَٰٓئِكَ عَلَىٰ هُدٗى مِّن رَّبِّهِمۡۖ وَأُوْلَٰٓئِكَ هُمُ ٱلۡمُفۡلِحُونَ

- (قلى) - Marks a permissible stop and it is *preferred to stop* (الوقف الجائز مع كون الوقف أولى):

  - ➢ It is your choice to stop or continue, but it is preferred to stop.

  - **Example:**

مَّا يَعۡلَمُهُمۡ إِلَّا قَلِيلٞۗ فَلَا تُمَارِ فِيهِمۡ

- (∴ ∴) - Those two sets of three dots mark two points where you ***can*** stop, but if you stop at one of them you should not stop at the other **(علامتا تعانق الوقف بحيث يصح الوقف فقط على إحداهما)** .

  - **Example:**

ذَٰلِكَ ٱلْكِتَٰبُ لَا رَيْبَ ۛ فِيهِ ۛ هُدًى لِّلْمُتَّقِينَ

- (س) - Marks a **Sakt** (**سكت**), where you pause your recitation and then continue. Note that when you pause for the Sakt, you don't breathe; it is just a quick pause **(علامة سكتة لطيفة بدون تنفس)** .

  - **Example:**

وَقِيلَ مَنْ ۜ رَاقٍ

Additional Signs

(Not included in all prints of the Qur'anic text)

- (ع) - Indicates **Ruku'** (ركوع), so if you are reciting the Qur'an in your Salah (prayer), this sign marks a good point to finish your recitation and make Ruku'. This sign marks the end of a group of Ayat that are related to each other, or the end of a story.

  - ➢ Note that this sign can be used as a daily mark if you want to memorize the whole Qur'an in 2 years.

(ع) علامة على الركوع (ع) للمصلي، فالمناسب له الركوع
عندها، لأنها إشارة إلى تمام المعني أوالقصة أو الموعظة ونحوها، وهي
الحصة اليومية لمن يريد حفظ القرآن في عامين إن شاء الله.

Snippet from the original "**Convention of Dabt Signs** (اصطلاحات ضبط المصحف)"

- **Example:**

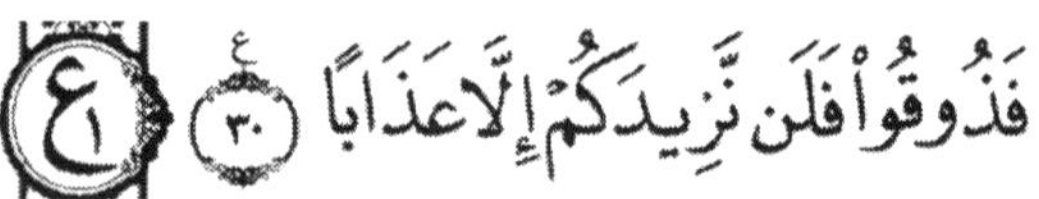

Note the number next to the letter (ع) which represents the number of the Ruku' since the Juz' has started; the first Ruku' has number (١), the second Ruku' has number (٢), and so on.

- **(السبع)** - Marks the end of a (Subu') or one-seventh of the Holy Qur'an. Each Subu' is labeled or numbered to show which Subu' it is. So (السبع الأول) marks the end of the first Subu', (السبع الثاني) marks the end of the second Subu', and so on.

(السبع) علامة الأسباع تدل على انتهاء السبع، وهي أيضاً دليلٌ لمن يختم في أسبوع.

Snippet from the original **"Convention of Dabt Signs (اصطلاحات ضبط المصحف)"**

- **Example:**

This sign marks the fifth Subu' (seventh) (السبع الخامس) of the holy Qur'an.

GLOSSARY

Ahadith (أحاديث)	Plural of Hadith (in Arabic).
Articulation Point (مخرج الحرف)	The point where the letter comes out when we pronounce it.
Aya (آية)	A verse of the Qur'an.
Ayat (آيات)	Plural of Aya (in Arabic) which is a verse of the Qur'an.
Dabt (ضبط)	Punctuation or making things precise.
Dumma (الضمة)	Dumma (ُ) is one of the Arabic short vowels. It sounds like a short (و).
Fat'ha (الفتحة)	Fat'ha (َ) is one of the Arabic short vowels. It sounds like a short (ا).
Full (Complete) Idgham (إدغام كامل)	A type of Idgham where a letter is merged into the next letter completely as if the first letter is totally dropped.
Ghunna (غنة)	A nasal sound (comes out when we pronounce the letters Noon or Meem (ن , م)).
Hadith (حديث)	A report attributed to the Prophet Muhammad (صلى الله عليه وسلم).
Hamza (همزة)	The Arabic letter (ء).
Hamzat-ulwasl (همزة الوصل)	The connecting Hamza: You pronounce it as a clear Hamza if it is at the beginning of the sentence, and you drop it when it is in the middle.
Haraka (حركة)	A Haraka (حركة) is either a Fat'ha (َ), a Dumma (ُ), or a Kasra (ِ), which are the short vowels in Arabic.

Harakat (حركات)	Plural of Haraka (in Arabic).
Hizb (حزب)	Half a Juz'.
Huroof Muqatta'a (الحروف المقطعة)	The letters at the beginning of some Suras of the Qur'an like (ألم or كهيعص).
Idgham (إدغام)	Merging a letter into the next one.
Ikhfa' (إخفاء)	Hiding a letter. (For the ن or م, it is done by replacing the letter with a Ghunna (nasal sound).
Ikhtilas (اختلاس)	Pronouncing the letter with a short Haraka
Imala (إمالة)	Pronouncing the Alif (ا) in a way between the original sound and the (ي).
Incomplete Idgham (إدغام ناقص)	A type of Idgham where the first letter is merged into the second letter, but the merging is not complete, so the first letter keeps some of its attributes.
Ishmam (إشمام)	Pronouncing the letter while rounding the lips as we do when pronouncing the Dumma (◌ُ), but no actual Dumma is pronounced (no Dumma sound).
Izhar (إظهار)	Showing and pronouncing the letter clearly.
Juz' (جزء)	One of the thirty parts, which the Qur'an is divided into.
Kasra (الكسرة)	Kasra (◌ِ) is one of the Arabic short vowels. It sounds like a short (ي).
Laam Atta'reef (لام التعريف)	Laam Atta'reef, and sometimes referred to as Al-Atta'reef (ال التعريف), is a Laam (ل) that is added to a noun to define it (make it definite).
Laam Qamariya (اللام القمرية)	One of the two cases of Laam Atta'reef where the Laam is pronounced clearly.

Laam Shamsiya (اللام الشمسيّة)	One of the two cases of Laam Atta'reef where the Laam is merged into the next letter (it is not pronounced).
Leen letter (حرف اللّين)	Leen letter is either a (و or ي) that has a Sukoon while the preceding letter has a Fat'ha (◌َ).
Madd (المدّ)	Lengthening or stretching the letters (ي , و , ا), which are called the letters of Madd.
Madd 'Arid Lissukoon (المد العارض للسكون)	Stretching the Madd letter when it is the second-to-last letter when you stop or pause your recitation.
Madd Lazim (المدّ اللازم)	Madd Lazim is to stretch the Madd letter when it is followed by a Sukoon (◌ْ) or a Shadda (◌ّ). It is stretched to 6 counts.
Madd Leen (مد اللّين)	Stretching the Leen letter when it is the second-to-last letter when you stop or pause your recitation.
Madd sign (~)	A sign placed on the Madd letter to indicate it should be stretched more than the original length of 2 counts.
Mus-haf (المصحف)	The book that contains the Holy Qur'an. So, the Mus-haf is the physical book that we can hold in our hands, while the Qur'an is the words of Allah that are written in the Mus-haf.
Qalb (القلب)	Converting Noon Saakina of (ن) into Meem (م).
Rawm (الروم)	Pronouncing the letter with a short Haraka when stopping on that letter.
Riwayat (رواية)	Narrated method of reciting the Qur'an.
Ruku' (ركوع)	Bowing down (like in Salah).
Saakin (or Saakina) Letter	A letter with Sukoon.

Sakt (سكت)	A short pause (without breathing) while reciting the Qur'an.
Shadda (الشّدة)	The Shadda (ّ) is a sign placed on a letter to indicate it is repeated twice; the first one has a Sukoon, and the second one has the Haraka that is displayed above or below the Shadda.
Sujood Attilawa (سجود التلاوة)	Doing prostration when reciting an Aya that has Sujood (Sajda).
Sukoon (سكون)	Sukoon (ْ) on a letter indicates the absence of Haraka (short vowels) on that letter; the letter is in a still position (no Haraka above or below it).
Sura (سورة)	A Chapter of the Qur'an.
Tajweed (التجويد)	Articulating every letter from its proper articulation point with the proper attributes while maintaining the rights and dues of each letter.
Tanween (التنوين)	A Noon (ن) sound that is added to the end of the word in certain circumstances (according to the Arabic grammar). It is represented by 2 Harakat (ٍ, ٌ, ً).
Tarteel (الترتيل)	To recite clearly in a measured way.
Tas-heel Al-Hamza (تسهيل الهمزة)	Pronouncing the Hamza in a way between the original sound of the Hamza (ء) and the sound of the Alif (ا).

Made in the USA
Middletown, DE
03 January 2025

68779211R00052